FINDING

INNER
PEACE

DURING

TROUBLED

TIMES

The Barnabas Agency

FINDING INNER PEACE DURING TROUBLED TIMES
Published by The Barnabas Agency, a division of The B & B Media Group, Inc.
109 S. Main St., Corsicana, TX 75110 U.S.A.
www.barnabasagency.com

ISBN: 978-0-578-04244-2

© William Moss 2009
LCCN: 2009912638

Author is represented by The B & B Media Group, Inc.,
109 S. Main, Corsicana, Texas 75110
1-903-872-0517
www.tbbmedia.com

Design: Lauri Worthington, Martino Creative
Eric Samuelson 2009, www.SamuelsonCreative.com

Recommendations for Finding Inner Peace During Troubled Times

"*Finding Inner Peace During Troubled Times* is a very special book because it was written by a person whose working life has been in the tough world of business and not someone in the ministry or whose vocation is spiritual direction."

JOHN C. DANFORTH *served as a United States Senator from Missouri for 18 years and is an ordained Episcopal priest. He is the author of* Faith and Politics *published by The Viking Press, a division of Penguin USA.*

"Bill Moss takes Jesus at his word, that he promises us inner peace in the here-and-now. Bill's authority comes from much prayer and study, many conversations, the crucible of suffering, and the experience of healing and hope. He gives us clear, credible guidance how to discover this gift of peace."

(THE REV.) CURTIS ALMQUIST, SSJE
SUPERIOR
The Society of Saint John the Evangelist, Cambridge, Massachusetts

"Bill Moss in *Finding Inner Peace During Troubled Times* invites us to join him in his pilgrimage into inner peace. Indeed, today, 'worry, self-preservation, hunger, lack of money, arrogance, competetiveness, criticism and illness' are frequently our constant companions, but Bill suggests that God's radical love in Jesus brings us into the mind of Christ. In our prayers he urges us 'to breathe in love, breathe out anger'. What a magnificent insight into God's love that Bill offers to us!

"I highly recommend this deeply spiritual book as a way for all of us to find inner peace."

THE REVEREND CANON JOHN L. PETERSON
Canon for Global Justice and Reconciliation, Washington National Cathedral

"This book is a gentle reminder that God is waiting for us to be at one with him in sincere and heartfelt prayer. Words are offered on each page to help us find our own words in which to express our deepest desires to God. We are then invited to listen in loving silence to all that God might want to share with us."

JAMES FINLEY, PH.D.
Author of Christian Meditation

"What a spiritually soothing book! The combination of scriptures works wonders – they are calming and reassuring. I couldn't quit reading it, and when I finished, I did feel at peace. This is a book our busy world needs."

RENA PEDERSON, *author of* What's Next? Women Redefining Their Dreams in the Prime of Life *and* The Lost Apostle, Searching for the Truth about Junia.

To my wife, Dianne,
whom I will love forever

✝ ACKNOWLEDGEMENT

I want to thank my good friend and spiritual advisor, The Reverend William J. A. Power, for encouraging me to write this essay. Bill Power changed the direction of my life with his wisdom, compassion, and understanding. I want to compliment him on his standing as an outstanding theological scholar, teacher and communicator. He has helped so many people in their search for a more meaningful life with Christ. His life is a window through which God's light shines.

I express my appreciation to my assistant, Mona Pollina, for her suggestions and dedication to this project.

TABLE OF CONTENTS

FOREWORD

Inner peace can be found
through prayer and meditation.

You can find a peace
that transcends all distractions.

God will lead you to a peace
emanating from the Holy Spirit.

A peace born of a constant
awareness of God's presence.
God's tranquility, love, beauty
and serenity.

Peace, like life, is a gift from God.
He will show us the path to follow.

THOUGHTS & PRAYERS

INNER PEACE

I recently talked during lunch with my spiritual advisor in Dallas about whether either of us had ever known anyone who had achieved real inner peace and how it might be possible to do so. We talked about the world before Christ's time, how nations started wars with sticks and stones, went to bows and arrows and from there to all of the destructive advances in sophisticated military equipment. How peoples' lives became more complicated. How inventions and science changed the way we do things. How competition has increased, finance is more complicated, education is less effective.

THOUGHTS & PRAYERS

We talked about how the population has increased, and the diversification of races, cultures and nations. There have been constant evolutions of productivity, transportation and communication. There are many scientific inventions, such as the atom bomb, which would create unimaginable damage. We talked about the arms race in the Middle and Far East, and that Israel, Pakistan, India, China, and North Korea, have nuclear capacity, which could lead to destruction beyond our comprehension.

THOUGHTS & PRAYERS

We talked about living in today's strange and changing world shaped by banking collapses, recessions, wars, politics, famine, hurricanes, pollution and diverse economies and demographics. How we deal with death and illnesses. How does this changing, strange world affect our daily decisions and where does God fit into all of this?

THOUGHTS & PRAYERS

●●●●●●●●●●●●●●●●●●●●●●●●●●

I believe God wants us to find peace and will
show us the way, if we are willing to accept
it. We discussed whether or not we might
isolate ourselves from the world around us
by withdrawing within ourselves in our
search for inner peace. Would we be selfish
because our withdrawal might preclude us
from being involved in the solutions of the
many problems that confront us? However,
if we search for inner peace, because we
want to share it, then we may be able to
help others. Inner peace, like life, is a gift
from God.

THOUGHTS & PRAYERS

✝ BIBLICAL WRITERS

It is evident that the biblical writers want us to find peace because the Psalmist says, "Turn from sin and do good; seek peace and pursue it."[1] In Romans Paul says, "Therefore, since we have been justified through faith, we have peace with God through our Lord Jesus Christ."[2] In Ephesians the author says, "For he himself is our peace, who has made the two one and has destroyed the barrier, the dividing wall of hostility."[3] In Colossians it says, "Let the peace of Christ rule in your hearts, since as members of one body you were called to peace."[4] In John Jesus says, "I have told you these things, so that in me you may have peace. In this world you will have trouble. But take heart! I have overcome the world."[5]

notes _____

[1] Psalm 34:14; [2] Romans 5:1; [3] Ephesians 2:14;
[4] Colossians 3:15; [5] John 16:33

THOUGHTS & PRAYERS

However, there are many difficulties,
distractions and hardships that stand in
the way of our inner peace.

As Paul said to the Galatians, "So I say,
live by the Spirit, and you will not gratify the
desires of the sinful nature. For the sinful
nature desires what is contrary to the Spirit
and the Spirit what is contrary to the sinful
nature. They are in conflict with each other,
so that you do not do what you want. But if
you are led by the Spirit, you are not under
laws of Moses."

THOUGHTS & PRAYERS

Paul says "that the acts of the sinful nature are obvious: sexual immorality, impurity and debauchery; idolatry and witchcraft; hatred, discord, jealousy, fits of rage, selfish ambition, dissensions, factions and envy; drunkenness, orgies, and the like." Today there are some distractions Paul did not include such as: worry, self preservation, hunger, lack of money, arrogance, competitiveness, criticism and illness, to name a few.

THOUGHTS & PRAYERS

Paul continues. "I warn you, as I did before, that those who live like this will not inherit the kingdom of God. But the fruit of the Spirit is by practicing love, joy, peace, patience, kindness, goodness, faithfulness, gentleness and self-control. Against such things there is no law. Those who belong to Christ Jesus have crucified the sinful nature with its passions and desires. Since we live by the Spirit, let us keep in step with the Spirit. Let us not become conceited, provoking and envying each other."[6]

Through prayer and meditation we can transcend all these distractions and difficulties if we live by the Spirit and put God's love and presence first.

notes _____

6 Galatians 5:15-26

THOUGHTS & PRAYERS

THE HOLY SPIRIT

God's Spirit is within us constantly. God's Spirit dwells in us and it is the core and center of our being at all times. As it says in John, "We know that we live in him and he in us because he has given us his spirit."[7] As Jesus says, "On that day you will realize that I am in my Father and you are in me and I am in you."[8] Jesus said, "The Kingdom of God does not come with your careful observation, nor will people say here it is or there it is, because the kingdom of God is within you."[9] Therefore, because God is in Jesus, Jesus is in you, and you are in God, the Holy Spirit can dwell in you at all times, and you are one with the Holy Spirit. Prayer and Christian meditation take on a completely different quality when we realize that God knows us intimately from within.

notes _____

[7] John 4:13; [8] John 14:20; [9] Luke 17:20-21

THOUGHTS & PRAYERS

I believe in one God as in Ephesians, "There is one body and one Spirit – just as you were called to one hope when you were called – one Lord, one faith, one baptism; one God and Father of all, who is over all and through all and in all."[10] I also believe that each of us can have a tiny piece of God that is all our own. I know I believe that to be true and God has let me believe it.

notes _____

[10] Ephesians 4:4-6

THOUGHTS & PRAYERS

GOD IS LOVE

In John Jesus says, "Dear friends, let us love one another, for love comes from God. Everyone who loves has been born of God and knows God. Whoever does not love does not know God, because God is love. This is how God showed His love among us: He sent His one and only Son into the world that we might live through Him. This is love: not that we loved God, but that He loved us and sent His Son as an atoning sacrifice for our sins. Dear friends, since God so loved us, we also ought to love one another No one has ever seen God; but if we love one another, God lives in us and His love is made complete in us.[11]

notes _____

[11] 1 John 4:7-12

13

THOUGHTS & PRAYERS

Jesus said, "You did not choose me, but I chose you and appointed you to go and bear fruit – fruit that will last. Then the Father will give you whatever you ask in my name. This is my command: Love each other."[12] Paul said to the Philippians, "Do not be anxious about anything, but in everything, by prayer and petition, with thanksgiving, present your requests to God. And the peace of God, which transcends all understanding, will guard your hearts and your minds in Christ Jesus."[13]

notes _____

[12] 1 John 4:7-12; [13] John 15:16-17

THOUGHTS & PRAYERS

God's love comes from within. Within God's love are the seeds for inner peace. When God helps us find our soul through love and we share that love with others, He is showing us a path to follow in our search for inner peace.

THOUGHTS & PRAYERS

SEEKING INNER PEACE

If we seek inner peace we will find it. In John Jesus says, "And I will do whatever you ask in my name, so that the Son may bring glory to the Father. You may ask me for anything in my name, and I will do it."[14]

notes _____

14 John 4:13-14

THOUGHTS & PRAYERS

Also in John, Jesus says, "All this I have spoken while still with you. But the Counselor, the Holy Spirit, whom the Father will send in my name, will teach you all things and will remind you of everything I have said to you. Peace I leave with you; my peace I give you. I do not give to you as the world gives. Do not let your hearts be troubled and do not be afraid."[15]

notes _____

[15] John 14:25-27

THOUGHTS & PRAYERS

ASPECTS OF PEACE

Can we find inner peace here on earth? Will
we be able to refuse all temptation? Can we
fully forgive and be truly forgiven? Can we
be humble rather than arrogant and self-
serving? Can we be understanding and have
compassion for others? Can we control our
temper? Can we be kind, gentle, patient
and helpful? Can we compete in a highly
competitive world where people slander us
and bear false witness? Can we live and
work in this materialistic world and find inner
peace? I believe we can if we clear our
minds of everything except God's love and
peace during prayer and Christian meditation;
if we turn our will and our lives over to the
care of God, and within our heart of hearts put
our faith and trust in His love and Holy Spirit.

THOUGHTS & PRAYERS

All the while thanking God for the many gifts, blessings, and directions He has given us through our lifetimes. We need to thank God for the abundant times He has provided for us. Recognizing the many gifts we have received and the comforts and joys of life He has provided us.

THOUGHTS & PRAYERS

Since the lunch with my spiritual advisor, I have come to the conclusion that through prayer and Christian meditation, faith and trust in God, Jesus Christ and the Holy Spirit, there is the opportunity to realize inner peace that will transcend all distractions. I believe that within the scriptures God has encouraged us to seek and pursue inner peace. If we pray for inner peace we will receive it.
A peace emanating from the Holy Spirit. A peace that shares beauty, tranquility, love and serenity. A peace born of a personal awareness of God's presence. An inner peace that will help us solve our problems.

THOUGHTS & PRAYERS

PRAYER & MEDITATION

Start prayer and meditation by finding a quiet comfortable place, by closing your eyes, by breathing deeply until you are completely relaxed. Quietly and slowly open your heart and mind to a loving God whose Spirit is dwelling within you.

Breathe in love; breathe out anger.

Breathe in peace; breathe out despair.

Relax; let God's love into your heart.

Be calm, be at peace, take more deep breaths, and feel the stress, anxiety and fear drain from your bodies.

THOUGHTS & PRAYERS

Be very quiet, completely relax your body and mind, breathe deeply and quietly several times and continue to listen while seeking conscious contact with God and continued awareness of His presence and love.

Accept God's love and feel the tranquility and the beauty of His love.

Turn your anxieties over to God. Accept things for just what they are.

THOUGHTS & PRAYERS

Everything is all right. "Remembering that all things work together for the good for those who love the Lord."[16]

I have asked for His direction; I believe I am where He wants me to be. I am comfortable; I am at peace. He has blessed me in so many ways. I am grateful for all that He has done for me.

Dear God, I pray that I can put my life in your hands and that you will grant me inner peace.

notes _____

16 Romans 8:28

THOUGHTS & PRAYERS

THE SPIRIT OF GOD

One constant thing that we can depend on in our lives, if we believe in God, and are willing to accept God, is that God's spirit and love will always guide us and support us through prayer and meditation, every hour of the day and night, every week and every month and every year until we meet Him in heaven.

THOUGHTS & PRAYERS

AFTERWORD

A friend who read this essay asked if I had received inner peace. The answer is yes. I am more peaceful and content now than I was nine months ago when the discussion of this essay began.

For me, finding inner peace through God's love and guidance continues to be an ongoing and cumulative process. The simplicity and tranquility of my peace continues to develop from within, while the world around me seems to become more and more complex and difficult to understand.

THOUGHTS & PRAYERS

It is normal for difficulties and problems to occur in our lives. It's not the problems but how we react to them that's important. When distractions occur I remind myself over and over again to be constantly aware of God's love and presence. By repeating the prayer and meditation throughout the day, a peace emanating from the Holy Spirit transcends all distractions and continues to grow within me. Inner peace is a gift from God. If our minds and hearts are open to accept this gift, God will show us the path to follow.

I believe Jesus when he said, "Whatever you ask for in prayer, believe that you have received it, and it will be yours."[17]

notes _____

[17] Mark 11:24

To learn more about the author,
go to www.williammoss.org.

Or to join William Moss' blog, go to
www.findingchristpeace.blogspot.com.